A
Short Guide
to a
Happy Life

A
Short Guide
to a
Happy Life

ANNA QUINDLEN

RANDOM HOUSE

NEW YORK

COPYRIGHT © 2000 BY ANNA QUINDLEN

All rights reserved.

Published in the United States by Random House,
an imprint and division of
Penguin Random House LLC, New York, and
simultaneously in Canada by Random House of
Canada Limited, Toronto.

RANDOM HOUSE and the HOUSE colophon are registered
trademarks of Penguin Random House LLC.

Originally published in hardcover in the United States
by Random House, an imprint and division of
Penguin Random House LLC, in 2000.

The excerpt from "Exhaust the little moment. Soon it dies,"
by Gwendolyn Brooks, which appears on page 25, is from *Blacks,*
by Gwendolyn Brooks (Chicago, Ill.: Third World Press, 1987).
Reprinted by the kind permission of Gwendolyn Brooks.

LIBRARY OF CONGRESS CATALOGING-IN-PUBLICATION DATA
Quindlen, Anna.
A short guide to a happy life / Anna Quindlen.
p   cm.
ISBN 9780593230473 (alk. paper)
ISBN 9780375506475 (ebook)
1. Conduct of life. I. Title.
BJ1581.2.Q56   2000
170'.44—dc21   00-25894

Printed in the United States of America on acid-free paper

randomhousebooks.com

2 4 6 8 9 7 5 3 1

2020 Random House Edition

Book design by Barbara M. Bachman

For Janet Maslin

A
Short Guide
to a
Happy Life

I'm not particularly qualified by profession or education to give advice and counsel. It's widely known in a small circle that I make a mean tomato sauce, and I know many inventive ways to hold a baby while nursing, although I haven't had the opportunity to use any of them in years. I have a good eye for a nice swatch and a surprising paint chip, and I have had a checkered but occasionally successful sideline in matchmaking.

But I've never earned a doctorate, or even a master's degree. I'm not an ethicist, or a philosopher, or an expert in any particular field. Each time I give a commencement speech I feel like a bit of a fraud. Yogi Berra's advice seems as good as any: When you come to a fork in the road, take it!

I can't talk about the economy, or the universe, or academe, as academicians like to call where they work when they're feeling kind of grand. I'm a novelist. My work is human nature. Real life is really all I know.

Don't ever confuse the two, your life and your work. That's what I have to say. The second is only a part of the first. Don't ever forget what a friend once wrote to Senator Paul Tsongas when the senator had decided not to run for reelection because he'd been

diagnosed with cancer: "No man ever said on his deathbed I wish I had spent more time at the office."

Don't ever forget the words on a postcard that my father sent me last year: "If you win the rat race, you're still a rat."

Or what John Lennon wrote before he was gunned down in the driveway of the Dakota: "Life is what happens to you while you're busy making other plans."

That's the only advice I can give. After all, when you look at the faces of a class of graduating seniors, you realize that each student has only one thing that no one else has. When you leave college, there are thousands of people out there with the same degree

you have; when you get a job, there will be thousands of people doing what you want to do for a living.

But you are the only person alive who has sole custody of your life. Your particular life. Your entire life. Not just your life at a desk, or your life on the bus, or in the car, or at the computer. Not just the life of your mind, but the life of your heart. Not just your bank account, but your soul.

People don't talk about the soul very much anymore. It's so much easier to write a résumé than to craft a spirit. But a résumé is cold comfort on a winter night, or when you're sad, or broke, or lonely, or when you've gotten back the chest X ray and it

doesn't look so good, or when the doctor writes "prognosis, poor."

Here is my résumé. It's not what my professional bio says, proud as I am of all that:

I am a good mother to three good children. I have tried never to let my profession stand in the way of being a good parent. I no longer consider myself the center of the universe. I show up. I listen. I try to laugh.

I am a good friend to my husband. I have tried to make my marriage vows mean what they say. I show up. I listen. I try to laugh.

I am a good friend to my friends, and they to me. Without them I would have nothing of interest to say to anyone, because

I would be a cardboard cutout. But I call them on the phone, and I meet them for lunch. I show up. I listen. I try to laugh.

I would be rotten, or at best mediocre, at my job if those other things were not true. You cannot be really first-rate at your work if your work is all you are.

So I suppose the best piece of advice I could give anyone is pretty simple: get a life. A real life, not a manic pursuit of the next promotion, the bigger paycheck, the larger house. Do you think you'd care so very much about those things if you developed an aneurysm one afternoon, or found a lump in your breast while in the shower?

Get a life in which you notice the smell

of salt water pushing itself on a breeze over the dunes, a life in which you stop and watch how a red-tailed hawk circles over a pond and a stand of pines. Get a life in which you pay attention to the baby as she scowls with concentration when she tries to pick up a Cheerio with her thumb and first finger.

Turn off your cell phone. Turn off your regular phone, for that matter. Keep still. Be present.

Get a life in which you are not alone. Find people you love, and who love you. And remember that love is not leisure, it is work. Each time I look at my diploma, I remember that I am still a student, still learning every day how to be human. Send

an e-mail. Write a letter. Kiss your mom. Hug your dad.

Get a life in which you are generous. Look around at the azaleas making fuchsia star bursts in spring; look at a full moon hanging silver in a black sky on a cold night. And realize that life is glorious, and that you have no business taking it for granted. Care so deeply about its goodness that you want to spread it around. Take the money you would have spent on beers in a bar and give it to charity. Work in a soup kitchen. Tutor a seventh-grader.

All of us want to do well. But if we do not do good, too, then doing well will never be enough.

Live by the words of this poem by Gwendolyn Brooks:

EXHAUST THE LITTLE MOMENT.
SOON IT DIES.

AND BE IT GASH OR GOLD
IT WILL NOT COME

AGAIN IN THIS IDENTICAL
DISGUISE.

Life is short. Remember that, too.

I've always known this. Or almost always. I've been living with mortality for decades, since my mother died of ovarian cancer when she was forty and I was nineteen. And this is what I learned from that experience: that knowledge of our own mortality is the greatest gift God ever gives us.

It is so easy to waste our lives: our days, our hours, our minutes. It is so easy to take for granted the pale new growth on an evergreen, the sheen of the limestone on Fifth Avenue, the color of our kids' eyes, the way the melody in a symphony rises and falls and disappears and rises again. It is so easy to exist instead of live. Unless you know there is a clock ticking. So many of us changed our lives when we heard a biological clock and decided to have kids. But that sound is a murmur compared to the tolling of mortality.

Maybe you have come to feel the way I

have. And you've come to feel that way for a very difficult or demanding reason. One day you were walking around worrying about whether you had anything to wear to a party and reminding yourself to buy Kitty Litter or toilet paper. And then you were in the shower lathering up, or you were lying on a doctor's table, or the phone rang. And your world suddenly divided, as my world did many years ago. It divided into "before" and "after."

"Before" for me was my freshman year of college, when I found myself able for the first time in my life to swear at meals and not be reprimanded, to go out at midnight and not have to tell anyone where I was

going. "After" was the beginning of what would have been my sophomore year, when I found myself out of school, making meat loaf and administering morphine in a development house in the suburbs.

It is amazing how much you can learn in one year. Just like Paul, who was knocked off his mule into the dust on the way to Damascus, and discovered God, I had a rude awakening. I'm not sure I learned anything much about mortality, or death, or pain, or even love, although in the years since, I have found that that one horrible year has given me a perspective on all those things I wouldn't otherwise have had.

"Before" and "after" for me was not just

before my mother's illness and after her death. It was the dividing line between seeing the world in black and white, and in Technicolor. The lights came on, for the darkest possible reason.

And I went back to school and I looked around at all the kids I knew who found it kind of a drag and who weren't sure if they could really hack it and who thought life was a bummer. And I knew that I had undergone a sea change. Because I was never again going to be able to see life as anything except a great gift.

It's ironic that we forget so often how wonderful life really is. We have more time than ever before to remember it. The men

and women of generations past had to work long, long hours to support lots and lots of children in tiny, tiny houses. The women worked in factories and sweatshops and then at home, too, with two bosses, the one who paid them, and the one they were married to, who didn't.

There are new generations of immigrants now, who work just as hard, but those of us who are second and third and fourth generation are surrounded by nice cars, family rooms, patios, pools—the things our grandparents thought only rich people had. Yet somehow, instead of rejoicing, we've found the glass half empty. Our jobs take too much out of us and don't pay enough. We're

expected to pick the kids up at preschool and run the microwave at home.

C'mon, let's be honest. We have an embarrassment of riches. Life is good.

I don't mean in any cosmic way. I never think of my life, or my world, in any big cosmic way. I think of it in all its small component parts: the snowdrops, the daffodils; the feeling of one of my kids sitting close beside me on the couch; the way my husband looks when he reads with the lamp behind him; fettuccine Alfredo; fudge; *Gone with the Wind, Pride and Prejudice*. Life is made up of moments, small pieces of glittering mica in a long stretch of gray cement. It would be wonderful if they came to us unsummoned, but particularly in lives as busy as the ones most of us lead now, that won't happen. We have to teach ourselves how to make room for them, to love them, and to live, really live.

I learned to live many years ago. Something really bad happened to me, something that changed my life in ways that, if I had had a choice, it would never have been changed at all. And what I learned from it is what, today, sometimes seems to be the hardest lesson of all.

I learned to love the journey, not the destination. I learned that this is not a dress rehearsal, and that today is the only guarantee you get.

I learned to look at all the good in the

world and to try to give some of it back, because I believed in it completely and utterly. And I tried to do that, in part, by telling others what I had learned, even though so many people may have thought I sounded like a Pollyanna. By telling them this: Consider the lilies of the field. Look at the fuzz on a baby's ear. Read in the back-yard with the sun on your face. Learn to be happy. And think of life as a terminal illness, because, if you do, you will live it with joy and passion, as it ought to be lived.

Anyone can learn all those things, out there in the world. You just need to get a life, a real life, a full life, a professional life, yes, but another life, too. School never ends. The classroom is everywhere. The exam comes at the very end. No man ever said on his deathbed I wish I had spent more time at the office.

I found one of my best teachers on the boardwalk at Coney Island many years ago. It was December, and I was doing a story about how the homeless suffer in the winter months. He and I sat on the edge of the wooden supports, dangling our feet over the side, and he told me about his schedule, pan-handling the boulevard when the summer crowds were gone, sleeping in a church when the temperature went below freezing, hiding from the police amid the Tilt-A-Whirl and the Cyclone and some of the other seasonal rides.

But he told me that most of the time he stayed on the boardwalk, facing the water, just the way we were sitting now, even when it got cold and he had to wear his newspapers after he read them. And I asked him why. Why didn't he go to one of the shelters? Why didn't he check himself into the hospital for detox?

And he stared out at the ocean and said, "Look at the view, young lady. Look at the view."

And every day, in some little way, I try to do what he said. I try to look at the view. That's all. Words of wisdom from a man with not a dime in his pocket, no place to go, nowhere to be. Look at the view. When I do what he said, I am never disappointed.

ANNA QUINDLEN is a novelist and journalist whose work has appeared on fiction, nonfiction, and self-help bestseller lists. She is the author of nine novels: *Object Lessons, One True Thing, Black and Blue, Blessings, Rise and Shine, Every Last One, Still Life with Bread Crumbs, Miller's Valley,* and *Alternate Side.* Her memoir *Lots of Candles, Plenty of Cake,* published in 2012, was a #1 *New York Times* bestseller. Her book *A Short Guide to a Happy Life* has sold more than a million copies. While a columnist at *The New York Times,* she won the Pulitzer Prize and published two collections, *Living Out Loud* and *Thinking Out Loud.* Her *Newsweek* columns were collected in *Loud and Clear.*

AnnaQuindlen.net

Facebook.com/AnnaQuindlen

A B O U T   T H E   T Y P E

This book was set in Perpetua, a typeface designed by the English artist Eric Gill, and cut by the Monotype Corporation between 1928 and 1930. Perpetua is a contemporary face of original design, without any direct historical antecedents. The shapes of the roman letters are derived from the techniques of stonecutting. The larger display sizes are extremely elegant and form a most distinguished series of inscriptional letters.